Sonnets and Sunshine

Jack Oats

Sonnets and Sunshine

For my grandchildren

Sonnets and Sunshine
ISBN 978 1 76109 151 3
Copyright © Jack Oats 2021
Cover images: *Fourteen Lines in a Sonnet* (front) and *Spectrum Filling Space* (back), paintings by Madeleine Kelly

First published 2021 by
GINNINDERRA PRESS
PO Box 3461 Port Adelaide 5015
www.ginninderrapress.com.au

Contents

Introduction	9
Resolve	11
Joy	11
To have tried and not quite made a haiku	11

Around Australia in <80 sonnets

On the face of it, a continent overrun by poems	15
Sonnet from the heart	16
Dingo	17
Oooh! Book Now. The Aussie Outback Spectacular	18
Ephemeral	20
Dajarra déjà vu	21
Silence	22
Opal Capital of the World	23
The Diamantina	24
Another dawn chorus	25
Lyndhurst – key species: chestnut-breasted whiteface	26
The coward of Coward Springs	28
Socialist's lament	29
For people	30
Carrion waving	31
A rant for the sesquicentenary of Goyder's Line	32
Mungo jigsaws	33
Kham Sin	34
Across the Hay Plains	35
Poppy's tortles	36
Spectacles	37
Climb every mountain	38
Dream cruise	39
Accompanying	40

Grey honeyeater	41
Dear Cairns mob	42
Reptilian agglomeration	44
Ghosts of Edith	45
Her gifts	46
Requited love atop Lady Barrington	47
Lakes Entrance	48
Feather-soft	49
Early bike trips	50
Waiting for the call	51
Words out of the blue	52
Paradise shared	53
Denham dolphins	54
An osprey's impression	55
On doubling	56
Divine presence	58
Dreaming at Ubirr	59
Sorry business	60
Flight behaviour	61
Slip slidin' away	64
Dirty business	65
Lord Howe Island	66
Winter surfer	67
April 2121	68
White house	69
Tree change, sea change	70
Port Arthur	71
The twitchers' guide to Christmas Isle	72
Here's to Petrarch: XXXX	74

Sunshine after days of rain

Sunshine after days of rain	77
Moorings	78
The Affair	80
Suburban birding	81
Seagulls gather	83
Forest after fire	84
Spotted a pardalote	87
Buddha and the sherry drinkers	88
Trekkers' horseman, Bhutan	89
The Fat Friar	90
Dawn chorus in the Cardiac Stepdown Unit	92
Here for work	95
Creation pondered at the clifftop	96
Emu's four-and-twenty lamentation	98
Sergeant Small	100
For Paul on his sixtieth birthday	101
Butterflying	102
My friend	103
Shepherd with ute	104
Old currency	106
Gardening list	108
Locally	109
Omniserpent song	110
Girter makes four prayers	112
Dear Weatherbeaten	113
Laments due to:	114
Acknowledgements	115
A dedication	117

Introduction

Sonnets and Sunshine is an amalgam of my next two collections, *Around Australia in Eighty Sonnets* and *Sunshine After Days of Rain*. Neither collection is finished but time and pragmatics dictate they be combined. Each collection arose from a challenge.

Ron Pretty, in *Creating Poetry*, reckons, 'no one worth their salt can claim to be a real poet until they've produced at least a successful sonnet or two'. Truth is, success is debatable, eighty was always going to be too many and the sonnet form was always going to be too restrictive. So what you get is a few Petrarchan and Shakespearean sonnets, a bit of iambic pentameter and occasional rhyme, a lot of what I call mock sonnet, some free verse and, mostly, the expediency of just fourteen lines. What appeals and seems archetypally Australian about the sonnet is the ever-ready contradiction to accompany each idea; the Plan B made before Plan A is fully formed; the tail with the head, as though life comes down to the toss of a penny.

As white fella travellers together for four decades, Her Majesty Queen Jean and I have known places mostly by their colonial labels. However, we've been witness to the increasing national awareness of Indigenous Australians and their multi-millennia history of place naming. For many of the sonnets, in a sincere attempt to acknowledge Indigenous nomenclature, I have attempted to ascribe a current acknowledgement of Country. 'Sonnet from the heart' shares with you my belief in Makarrata and my hope for Australia to become a republic with a new flag, anthem and an indigenous head of state. Imagine our great pride and joy.

Bruce Dawe gave us *Sometimes Gladness*. I've taken this as

a challenge to counter each dirge I write with at least one gladness poem, my Sunshine poems. So easy to be overcome with inhumanity and environmental catastrophe even when we're surrounded by kindliness, beauty and good old-fashioned awe. Our lives, built with so many blocks. Our history, the childhood blocks (did we ever grow out of those?), the constructing and occasional abandonment of family homes, the constant maintenance of sustaining friendships. Blocks discarded, blocks renovated, blocks that remain our mainstays and blocks yet to be sculptured are the lives we each build and share; there is much about which to be glad.

Resolve

With each new day comes
resolve to sculpture anew
the block we call life.

Joy

Chip off the old block;
sample of abundant joy
you can make from life.

To have tried and not quite made a haiku

Late summer cicada
claws atop the block pile,
shrills unreservedly:
Ah! To be done with life.

Around Australia in <80 sonnets

On the face of it, a continent overrun by poems

Where the arteries congregate, black scabs
of printing as though font, style and boldness
matter, especially round the edges;
also featuring anatomical
curiosities, beauty spots, highlights.

Elsewhere, trampled by pink highlighter, most
of the arteries bleed onto the skin.
But strewth! Vast expanses of wrinkled crust
show only the thin tortured veins and blue
varicose splodges called ephemeral.

Herewith the Land of Oz (like Norman Gunston's
face sporting Tally-ho flags stuck to
fake shaving cuts). Cartography girt by sea
with Post-it markers waving victory.

Sonnet from the heart

Mutitjulu and Uluru in Northern Territory – country of Anangu,
Pitjantjatjara, Luritja and Yankuntjatjara Peoples

The sonnet suits genocide. Ancestors
dodged arsenic in the flour to pass down laws
of Country to an old man whose vivid
dream kills off the last Mutitjulu kid,
her brain fried from petrol-sniffing. Elsewhere,
descendants thrive, become leaders and dare
to cure the toxic silence, clear the debt,
bring optimism to the last couplet.

The sonnet gives reconciliation.
Makarrata* is the culmination
of the agenda; sing along to
a home-grown anthem called Uluru.
And imagine, imagine the weight
of an indigenous Head of State.

*From the Uluru Statement from the Heart, 2017

Dingo

West MacDonnell Ranges in Northern Territory – country of Arrernte People

She reads the signs
DON'T FEED DINGOS KEEP FOOD SECURE
each camp site scanned for traces
one ear jagged, one pointed

Every scent a murder clue
wiry pacing
patience blends into spinifex then back again
systematic across the hot afternoon

The pounce, keen jaws
into feral cat's shabby fur
with broken neck it's thrown in the air
dead before it hits the ground
discarded where it died. She trots away
tracks straight, well satisfied

Oooh! Book Now. The Aussie Outback Spectacular

Watarrka in Northern Territory – country of Luritja People

1

Google Outback, adventure awaits you.
Thinking red kangaroo? Hop online. Pay
with plastic. Uluru's too good to be true.
Leave your cares; shoot through with someone special.

Park the Land Cruiser at Blue Emu, enjoy
the view as you fly to the Red Centre;
the Outback Magazine has a review
of Forester and Outback Subaru.

THIS HIRE CAR MAY NOT BE DRIVEN OFF ROAD!
Join the pre-dawn queue to the SHEILAS loo,
as Outback Spirit coachloads do before
heading out from the All New Luxury
Outback Experience Resort, to walk
the canyon, once the curfew is lifted.

2

Or stop at the Park Entrance.*
                              Walk into
mulga until spinifex pigeons applaud
and rock wallabies stamp their approval,
then stepping lightly over lichens,
follow down to the lone mallee,
gather her fallen twigs, boil a billy.

Eat chocolate, stay quite still, inwardly
laugh at the little jacky lizard whose
spiky head angles backwards forwards where
a web-held gum leaf twists the shaded air.

As afternoon gives way, the sharing ants
will abandon your outback experience.
From a dry sandy creek bed, worry the stars;
they resolve earthly and cosmic affairs.

* With thoughts of 'The Glug Quest', C.J. Dennis

Ephemeral

Lake Bennett, Newhaven Sanctuary in Northern Territory – country of Ngalia-Warlpiri and Luritja Peoples

This is where hot air blasts over crusted salt
and two-years-worth of rain falls all at once.

Red dust follows the Troopy* through mulga,
skirts hard rock plateaus and massive dunes.

Seven of us edge this varicose splodge
on the map; more expansive than Port Jackson.

Rare as night parrots, we gaze, strip, walk; wade
hundreds of metres down the road, scattering

hatchlings of shield shrimp and fingerling fish.
Thigh deep we sink, we float. We're floating specks

dwarfed by sky, surrounded by spinifex,
saltbush and sand. I wear my specs. Every

detail a *dreamy bliss*.† We hold our breath.
And afterwards, billy tea quietly.

---

* Toyota Landcruiser troop carrier
† After 'Never Give All the Heart', W.B. Yeats

Dajarra déjà vu

Dajarra in Queensland – in country near Kalkadoon, Warluwarra
and Yalarrnga Peoples and home of the Dajarra Rhinos AFL Club

those odd unwashed-looking
white fellas eating baked beans
out of a can with their
tent in the dirt
on the Rhinos footy field
(don't ask)
right near the amenities block
that's been blocked for months, eh
they had to use the school toilets
embarrassed to walk past
the laughing mob
doing craft with Uncle teaching
them to make boomerangs
and having fits calling
them sticks
when they didn't work

and the unlucky kids
had to leave early
and walk for miles with Aunty
looking for bush tucker treats
when the shop's got lots
of chocolates and proper lollies

maybe Aunty'll cadge a lift
for 'em all back to town
in the white fellas' car
if it don't break down, eh

Silence

Strzelecki Creek in South Australia – country of Pirlatapa and Yandruwandha Peoples

The brush of a zephyr stirs spinifex,
on starlit tracks busy rodents scamper,
neighbourly howling from distant dingoes
and a spotted nightjar's weird *cook ook ook*.
Ubiquitous buzz of unknown insects,
the sharp crack of car metal contracting.
Miles above, jet mumblings taper away.
The campfire hesitates, hisses and glows.

Between sounds, anticipation expands
comfortably into night. It's freezing
but there's no threat in the darkness. Each pulse
of calm brings reverence for the wilderness.
The touch of your hand says we can suspend
breathing, listen to our lust, sit and wait.

Opal Capital of the World

Cooper Pedy in South Australia – country of Arabana and Kokatha Peoples

having driven thousands of kilometres, we
might have stopped, window-shopped
for knick-knacks or jewellery,
admired the subtle and the garish gem-stone settings,
the pendants on chains delicate, bold, discrete,
one with a glint of crimson like wet blood
another shining maroon-purple-blue-green
like opalescent bruising
or discovered some local oddments,
interacted with motley townsfolk

but a woman in the main street
staggering ahead of a drunkard
his voice and fist raised
told us not to bother

The Diamantina

Diamantina National Park in Queensland – country of Karuwali People

In the tortured desert where night parrots flew
from the claws of feral cats
to be barbed on fences; and bilbies fled,
their burrows trampled flat,
hoteliers salved cattlemen,
their glasses and hopes raised high
to the rain and the wealth and the barmaid…
that never came by.

So the termites
salvaged what they could
leaving monuments of iron,
the glint of smashed glass,
the pastoral shards,
the mile-wide stock route lines.

Another dawn chorus

Sturt National Park in New South Wales – country of Pirlatapa and Wadigali Peoples

A winter-crisp silence
expands the horizon.
Red kangaroos silhouetted
still and tall, ears twitching.
Hovering kestrels listen in a void
for the movement of shadows.
A wagtail waits low on a mulga-bush.
Woodswallows huddle breathless on a baton

anticipating the first glimmer
of a piano concerto;
Brahms's second comes to mind.
In one frozen moment
the desert greets the sun
the silence is done.

Lyndhurst – key species: chestnut-breasted whiteface*

Lyndhurst in South Australia – country of Kuyani People

Weary from long roads, sleepless nights on rough
ground fretting over long-haired rat plagues and
having dreamed the cinnamon quail-thrush and
thick-billed grasswren at sunrise, with enough

lethargy to remain on their camp chairs,
they assume the passive cake and coffee
ritual of sheer inactivity
and sure enough, three birds hopping in their

direction, curtsy atop low bluebush
displaying white faces and chestnut breasts
before disappearing over a crest.
The twitchers dream on in the pre-dawn hush…

but wait, that ringing bell is their alarm;
an urgent dawn, calls them from their tent-dreams
to boot-slog twelve miles accompanied by teams
of flies, profuse sweat and thoughts of self-harm

until awestruck by The Bird. Quest fulfilled,
they gawk then do a little victory dance
and in retelling, add to the romance,
saying, 'their song's a silvery tinkling bell

and strolling the rolling hills was good fun.'
Another twitchers' rite of passage won.

*As per *The Complete Guide to Finding the Birds of Australia* (Thomas *et al*. CSIRO Publishing, 2011)

The coward of Coward Springs

Coward Springs in South Australia – country of Arabana People

When grey nomads with sundowners observed
a weedy bloke, the sort you mightn't trust,
arrive with royalty, they strained and perved
as the pair set up their tent in the dust.

Conversations drifted back to where ya been
and where ya goin' and the plague of rats
and the price of diesel is obscene and
bashings and how to poison feral cats.

At stroke of midnight,* the many-long-dead
awoke to screaming, hiccough sobs and cries.
Burrowing rodents had sought her warm bed.
Weedy saved her but to dodge blaming eyes

by dawn he'd absconded with his princess;
not guilty but a coward ne'er the less.

*From 'The Four Ages of Man', W.B. Yeats

Socialist's lament

Tree of knowledge, Barcaldine in Queensland – country of Iningai People

1891 by an old gum tree,
it's time the striking shearers all agree.

In '72 it was time again:
we elected Gough, our own mighty man.

In '84 comrades from Wollongong came
to pay homage but nothing stays the same.

The knowledge tree, the ALP – their fate:
white-anting, political glyphosate

and Kevin-07 with $5 mil to spend
announcing beginnings, marking the end.

In a brief hiatus Julia shone
planted a knowledge-tree clone then was gone.

Now a sculptured wooden coffin plays host
to what's lost and a heritage-listed gum ghost.

For people

Carnarvon National Park in Queensland – country of Gayriri and Bidjara Peoples

Most of the resting bones of the ancients,
wrapped in bark, interred in nooks
along sandstone escarpment walls,
became trophies for colonial settlers.
Others removed to the 'safety' of public museums.
Fragment of fibula, splinters of spirit left to languish.

At 'Cathedral Cave', an interpretation sign says,
'fragile remnants of a vanishing culture' and
'the most abundant rock carving at this site
is that of the human vulva.

The significance of this motif is not known.'
We hurry the ten kilometres back to our tent
and confirm the warm strength, the enduring significance
linking millennia of generations.

Carrion waving

Warren in New South Wales to Cunnamulla in Queensland –
country of Wiradjuri, Wailwan and Wangaibon Peoples

Floating further outback,
the tail-tilting of black kites
replaces the scavenging of crows;
less shade, fewer grey roos
and more reds; the huge males
and their mates, blue fliers
Mum called them. Said the ear twitching
is their way of waving.

By the roadside or slumped
mid-highway where car drivers
swerve to avoid the carnage,
hit by shock waves from each road train,
the occasional kanga's ear flaps
as if to say, g'day!

A rant for the sesquicentenary of Goyder's Line

A believer built his house upon
the rock platform at low tide and…

A grazier fenced her herd on a floodplain and…

Houses were built on bushy ridgelines with
amazing vistas of approaching wildfires and…

1865, the bureaucrat drew a line in the sand:
a foot of rain a year is not enough to grow crops.
After a few good years
the Waste Lands Alienation Act* was repealed.
Rain did not follow the plough,
saltbush never returned;
ruined limestone buildings stun the deserted land.

And still we hear, flood-proof, fireproof, drought-proof,
while all we yearn is denial-proof, foolproof.

* in South Australia

Mungo jigsaws

Mungo in New South Wales – country of Paakantji, Muthi Muthi and Ngiyampaa Peoples

A central clearing in the grassy woodland on the lunette;
tall black figures with white ochre stripes
surround bones and ash.
Behind, naked children. Some watch the burial.

To the right, down by the shore, a kangaroo with joey;
the artist thought them safe from spears for the occasion.
Just beyond a high shell midden: Land Rover (1960s) and
a professorial type with shovel. He's a C-14* man.
Further right: a locked gate, two four-wheel drive mini-coaches
proclaiming

> *Paakantji*
> *Muthi Muthi*
> *Ngiyampaa*
> *Adventure*
> *Tours*

The top left, mists into Gondwanan ferns, palms, conifers.
Cleverly, on the reverse side, a flattened lunascape
with futuristic flying machines surrounding
bone, shell and plastic; a thousand fragments in a dust storm.

---

* C-14 (^{14}C) is the carbon isotope used in radiocarbon dating of organic material from archaeological studies.

Kham Sin

Whitsundays in Queensland – country of Giya People

A day of naked tropical sunshine
then, 'winds strengthening to gale force'.
Our bobbing saucer drags its anchor;
we're saved when real yachties throw us a line.
Endless days of rain, horizontal in sheets.
'Nara Inlet is your safest anchorage.'

On the two-way, the hire company insists
we return, although Whitsunday Passage
is all whipped-up egg whites. We motor
into standing waves, the tidal rip and fear;
become the flying saucer under sail.
Sometimes over the waves, sometimes through.

Can't wait to do it all again, though!
Yo-ho, yo-ho, bare boat sailing we will go!

Across the Hay Plains

Hay Plains of New South Wales – country of Wiradjuri People

Our minds jumpy as kangas at dawn,
we leave sunrise and Narrandera behind.
One tea, one coffee poised in cup holders;
cruise control set at a hundred and five
to keep pace with the semis. Their highway.

Tooting scares the crows. No worrying for
Barcoo bantams on floodplains, it's drought time;
dust puffs from padding sheep. Scanning. Staring.
Harmonic tyre-thrum. Three hours to Balranald.

No radio, no distraction; a pretence
of conversation, 'so tranquil,' 'so flat'.
Increasingly twitchy, jumping at shadows

and fixated on the prize – an éclair
for the first to spot the old man emu!

Poppy's tortles

Heron Island in Queensland – country of Gureng Gureng and Bayali Peoples

For Poppy. We met on holidays and joked that we could call each other 'Poppy'.

She frowns a seven-year-old's wide-eyed face
of concentration and teaches herself
snorkelling. Within ten minutes she has
outgrown the pool and leads me to the sea
where we float above multicoloured fish.
Later I explain about bleached coral.

She rescues confused hatchlings from around
the resort, carries them to the lagoon,
assures them the reef sharks and stingrays are
harmless, laughs when their flippers dangle off
her palm and I say she's grown tortle fingers,
cries when they're plucked up and carried off by
hungry gulls, squeals and cheers and claps when they
dive on her command and swim to freedom.

Spectacles

Hastings Point in New South Wales – country of Bundjalung People
Unearthed an old diary (commentary added decades later)

pre-dawn busy bodies	(euphemism?)
with 3 green prawns, caught 2 whiting	(hunter gatherer!)
skinny-dip estuary sunrise	(daring)
dress for breakfast	
one fresh fish each	(deep envy)
Council blokes arrive, stop work	(before they start?)
thermoses, tea, watch us swim	(lazy pervs)
pack tent, canoe; cold outdoor shower	
Her Majesty strips, shampoos, towels	
Me – 'Council blokes were impressed'	(one lit a fag
HM – 'they were ten miles away'	put wrong end in mouth)
Me – 'ten yards more like it'	(another bit side out of cup)
HM drove happily	(made to wear her glasses)
done with her morning's diablerie	

Climb every mountain

Kosciuszko in New South Wales – country of Ngarigo People

The day our granddaughter's results are due, we chat
in clear air from chair-lift to mountain top,
remark on the granite with its cold colours,
the possibility of pygmy possums under the boardwalk
and corroboree frogs breeding in the spring rills.
Rhomboid wombat poos on alpine mosses;
we want thylacines too,
they could hunt the feral brumbies.

On our return, the sky turns overcast, threatening
to freeze the knees off a class of school kids.
Dawdling over glasses of Kosciuszko Pale Ale
we compare biodiversity conservation and
alpine treks to matriculation exams.
Waiting for her call; hoping she has passed.

Dream cruise

From Sydney – country of Eora People, to Melbourne – country of Woiworung People

My afternoon nap features a *Princess
Adventure*. From Circular Quay, miracles
of familiar landmarks in sunset colours.
For days, becalmed, beyond bliss, the Pacific
Ocean gazing at our private balcony.
Elsewhere on board, obesity production
lines dull our appetites.
                          At Port Melbourne
we queue with rain-soaked workers waiting to
pack morning trams.
                          Then a blur of stewards,
marches us back to the ship! We're captives
of the disaffected Malaysian crew.

I wake with Covid fever and the ghost
of a cruise liner anchored in sea mist
at my window.
                          An early whiskey, please.

April 2020, near Port Kembla where the ill-fated Covid-carrying *Ruby Princess* was eventually berthed with a thousand crew trapped on board.

Accompanying

Wiluna in Western Australia – country of Martu People

A Petrarchan's easier than closing
the gap. Not talking assimilation
nor journeys. Reconciliation
is what's needed. Don't want pollies posing
with interventions. Redfern is city
but issues are the same in the outback.
Start with truth-telling along every track;
walking together. Not talking pity.

Talking history, justice. Social programs,
health workers, they're just a part of making
amends. Charity gives guilt and anguish;
generosity shows who gives a damn
and kindness builds some trust.
                              Just thinking:
could we all be speaking a bit of language.

The idea of accompanying was encapsulated by Leigh Sales in *Any Ordinary Day* (Penguin, 2019).

Grey honeyeater

Karijini in Western Australia – country of Banyjima, Kurrama and Innawonga Peoples

This small pale species,
its local name given us by Banyjima people,
a grandmother, her granddaughter
wishing luck, smiling.

And finally, the bird
feeding on mistletoe nectar
in the mulga, *Acacia anura*.
We mask our tears with steaming coffee;
grins as wide as the continent.
Our tick list of all seventy-three
Australian honeyeaters is complete!

Ignoring the wave of Wittenoom ghosts,
the KEEP OUT signs at iron ore and gold mines,
we'll drive our memories
the five thousand kilometres home
then raise a glass
to the gorge carved through red rock
and the soft chatter of women sharing their *Jirrunypa*.

Dear Cairns mob

From Canberra – country of Ngunnawal People, to Cairns –
country of Yidinjdji People

G'day cousins
                      Ah! To see you strutting
on that ABC *Back Blocks* show we adore.
A century of heritage-squawking
in suburban Cairns! Congrats! We loved your

'We're more Australian than the Holden car;
loftier than Bartle Frere.' You've been
champions of the rambling verandas
in old-style guest houses and classic Queenslanders

with their shady under-the-house.
And good on you for not being conned by
high-rise or climate deniers. You roused
on sea-sick mobs for believing the lies

of spruikers, when really the coral is stuffed.
Brazen and stylish, you swaggered between
bronzed bodies strewn about the Lagoon, puffed
with pride watching your grandkids make the scene

around the water features and caused trouble
along the Esplanade with the punters.
We avoid the trappings* of the Bubble
in Canberra. We remain bargain hunters

but increasingly, government ignores
minorities unless they're cashed up!
                                    Yours…

* https://www.mynabird.com.au/

Reptilian agglomeration

Kimberley in Western Australia – country of Ngarinyin People

Each has the other in a death grip but
the python has the upper hand! They roll
and the lizard is further constricted.
At sunrise, the victim gasps; a few
asp scales froth from its mouth. Golden brown,
the sand goanna stares at fate. Tongue to tongue,
snake jaws strike. The lizard's face shoved into
its coffin, the python's black face folded
back over its own eyes as prey is fed to
predator.
           At sunset, the goanna
distorts the slow acid bath of the snake's gut.
Snake's eyes stare at the tail end of its meal.

Elsewise, twelve foot of sleek snake is glinting
silver-white with a faint black patterning.

Ghosts of Edith

Edith Falls in Northern Territory – country of Jawoyn People

Missing
> mature spinifex
> habitat for grasswrens
> grasswrens
> wallaby pad, now a concrete pathway
> best camp site beneath trees where new kiosk stands
> remoteness after miles of dusty driving
> dirt roads
> swimming alone
> solitude
> father's hat, with him floating in its shade
> mother's coy smile under her hat
> their camp site, replaced by DAY VISITORS ONLY
> curlews' camp site, now featuring brick ablutions block
> DRINKING WATER downstream from the main pool
> campfire
> campfire cooking
> caring about snakes while collecting firewood
> wondering about crocodiles
> wonderment

Appreciating
> memories
> old photos
> stamina to explore beyond

Her gifts

Cape York Peninsula in Queensland – country of Lamalama,
Kunjen and Kokowarra Peoples and the golden-shouldered parrot

All four kids was 'ad unda that tin roof
Neva 'ad ta go ta 'ospital with any ov'em
An' all bought up on that dirt floor
New place wasn't built till they all left 'ome
And set up for theirselves
Mostly scattered south'a Cairns
One's farmen up the road about fifty kays
Nice t'ave some grandkids so close by
Good cattle country this if ya know it

Do the parrots meself, eh
They'd be gorn if it wasn't
For doen the little burns to bring on the grasses
And putten seed out for 'em in-between-times
And 'ere's somethen for ya trip

remembering her leathered face
sinewy brown arms gently outstretched
with big gnarled hands cupping fresh chook eggs
brings a teary warmth

Requited love atop Lady Barrington

Barrington Tops in New South Wales – country of Worimi and Biripi Peoples

With gasping breath and thudding heart we quest
Ignoring pains that stab and doubts that call
Each man with lust for her will do his best
To blaze the trail, to conquer by nightfall.

Our world – each twinge of consciousness – is strapped
And shouldered. Razor sweat on nail-scratched back.
With loin's dull ache, mind numb, our fate is mapped
Each thorn-etched face now trudges up her track.

Our trembling limbs cry out, we breast the peak
Tormented miles of climbing, suddenly done.
Desire quenched, in packs our spirits seek
The walkers raise a glass. The climb was fun.

And have you mused: life's mountains are a spoof?
Then take this earnest sonnet as your proof.

Lakes Entrance

Lakes Entrance in Victoria – country of Kurnai People

In the waves of time, you were not a lake with an entrance and it was a long walk to the sea and one could continue walking all the way to what is now called Tasmania. Before then, before Gondwana drifted into separate bits on underworld waves, walkers…whew, they could walk through waves of evolution.

Imagine, in these times of rising sea levels, you see a wave approaching your breakwater; a huge crashing sort of wave with the spume flying back to tell the next wave about the entrance ahead and the channel-dredge and the pretty-coloured little boats and all the sheds to flood along today's shore.

The locals claim to belong with you. They clean up after storm waves and dream about calm seas.

Tourists surge in summer, dribble through in winter. They bob along on swells; some like gulls, some like discarded polystyrene burger boxes.

The tidal people swash in to visit their kind: their friends, demons and ghosts. They recede but you'll welcome them back.

Feather-soft

Murray River, Berri in South Australia – country of Meru People

Becalmed under ancient spreading red gums;
chilled with riesling at sunset. They're single
until an errant belly-feather sparks
fine ripples. The pelican lifts, strokes warm
air, settles to glide over the river.

Next, a novice. Aerodynamically
challenged, it stalls, flaps, splashy water-walks.
She laughs. He dies for love. And just as quick,

pelican after mirrored pelican;
each crescent belly toward reflection
belly. Undercurrents rise until light
and wine seep into the grace of twilight,
leaving a certainty about flying
and desire for feather-soft touching.

To be read with Mozart's 21st Piano Concerto, Andante movement

Early bike trips

A Kawasaki 750 is
an unlikely start to a sonnet or
an affair. Her offer of the spare bed
was euphemistic. Thereafter, many
a mirror reflected discarded boots,
undoings of buttons and blemishes.
Many many smiles were made. Such is lust.

And no matter how still they sat, how smooth
the highway, the motor hummed and the clothes
teased at a hundred miles an hour;
the best part being how she squeezed in tight
on the pillion behind him, their helmets
clonking when her eyes closed, having regard
only for the moment. Such is trust.

Waiting for the call

Esperance in Western Australia – country of Wudjari People

'Back in the day,'
is now a piss-take of the cliché.
But it's true!
Back in the day, all one had to do
was globe-chat and dream,
idle over state borders and scheme;
buy a return flight on the net,
catch the next jet.

In Esperance, we took the call.
Invitation secured, we did all
of the above and more.
Drove 3,500 kilometres door to door,
unpacked, repacked; hid key under mat
and headed off to England, just like that.

Words out of the blue

Nullarbor in Western Australia – country of Mirning People

A sonnet is the perfect place for
following directions down a track
until it peters out in bluebush;
to feel the absence of concrete, gods,
fences, telecommunication
towers, overhead jets, truck rumblings;
to taste fresh air.

Calibrate the blueness of sky from
one horizon to the other,
wait for sunset without time or
the internet, smell night's mellow curl
of smoke from the cooking fire, stare until
heaven, saturated with starlight,
has no place for words.

Paradise shared

Perth in Western Australia – country of Wajuck People

They make you feel comfortable, as real as
family and like they'll see you in Heaven,
although their guide says one has to believe
to gain admittance. Perhaps they've been told
of a parallel paradise for upright
ardent atheists. You wonder about
other faiths, other parallels.

                      'Oh no
madam/sir, not Cloud Nine. Yours is Cloud Eight/
Seven/Six…with the other atheists/
Buddhists/Muslims/Hindus et cetera.
And it's Cloud Two for the Agnostics.
Ha ha! Yes, that's it, a flutter each way.'

All that's to come. Today you're with them in Perth
knowing you're most loved and welcome here on Earth.

'I've always felt that there was something pathetic in the founders of a religion who made it a condition of salvation that you should believe in them.' *The Razor's Edge,* Somerset Maugham (Doubleday, 1944).

Denham dolphins

Shark Bay Marine Park in Western Australia – country of Malkana People

Every day we amuse bus-loads of tourists.
Knee-deep, they poke a few token fish at us.
Our Elders say we'll learn not to be stupid
and greedy; we'll hear the squeaky tunes of
little birds complaining about their dull
spinifex world with its rare flash of colour
and appreciate our smooth water world.

They don't know why they call it Monkey Mia
but down they come from trees around the car park
and visitors centre, corralled like schools
of fish into the shallows by backpackers
with their skimpy white uniforms, tanned skins,
foreign accents, 'Y'all have a nice day,'
noisy with laughter. We are not amused.

An osprey's impression

Ningaloo Reef in Western Australia – country of Malkana People

Inshore, the ocean changes: purple hues,
deep blues and greens of morning then through
the day till gold and crimson. Beneath, in
modest gardens, tiny fish swarm; somehow
swirling colour-crazed bodies never bump.
Larger fish hang around tall coral crowns.
Turtles, sharks, manta rays saunter their rounds.

At midday, intensity of sparkle
increases with the distance from the shore.
Beyond the reef, tourist boat reflections
and diving terns tell of whale sharks. They lull
in liquid silver under spotter planes.

Onshore, red dust disturbs dull shrubs that scratch
each other. All one can do is wait, fast, watch.

On doubling

Broom in Western Australia – country of Jukun People

1

Rainfall and 'rithmetic's perfect for some
sonnetry. Let me explain. The year we
went to Broome in July, I was called dumb
for not packing a raincoat. But you see,

the hundred-year mean precipitation
for July was just two millimetres.
Even two hundred mils inundation
in a single month is bugger-all litres.

In fact, point zero-six-four-five-two mils
on every one of those three thousand and
more July days is the likely no rills,
no-frills scenario. In the Top End

a dry July is to be expected.
At this point, poets will have detected

2

that the Bard's nifty sonnet formula
for lines and rhymes, like him, has expired
before the story's end. And you'll allow,
his iambic pentameter is mired.

Rush on then to this weather event of
the first three days in July twenty-ten
when the heaven's outpourings were above
the past century's total and then

some. Being used to cyclones, Broome managed,
but prayed for ninety-nine years without rain
to restore the two-millimetre average.
Someone asked, if you were going again,

would you take a raincoat? Well probably no!
The Kimberley? Dry July's the time to go.

Divine presence

Mitchell Plateau in Western Australia – country of Worrora,
Wunambal-Gamber and Ngarinyin Peoples

Hearing Kings College Choir (established 1441),
reading their names (Anne Boleyn, Henry VIII)
in the Chapel at Cambridge and it's nearly happening.
Again in Spain, the deep crypt at Arantzazu,
stepping over lives inscribed on tombstones,
breathing air as old as the Basque
but not really our sort of gods.

Nothing happening beyond the pay turnstiles at Stonehenge
nor in cathedrals, colonnades, porticos with their nativities.
And Egyptian mummies at the Musei Vaticani
pleasing what sort of gods?

Rock art galleries at Ngauwudu
going back ten, twenty, thirty thousand years and
god, it's happening.

Dreaming at Ubirr

Ubirr in Northern Territory – country of Bininj People

The Artist, my eldest, is back at the shelter
preoccupied with painting; forgetting to tend the fire.
The other children are my floodplain conspirators.
We wait in ambush for the large buck to graze closer.
They reappear/disappear in lush swamp vegetation;
their mesmerising death dance silently corrals
the kangaroo within spearing distance.
Later we'll eat and curse as we scratch our leech and insect welts.
The waiting drives me crazy.

                        Overlooking
three thousand generations
and hazy millennia of the changing land,
my meditation with the ancestors is busted
by the next punter rush to the lookout.
A fading dream: I'll come back as an artist not a hunter.

Sorry business

Nhulunbuy Airport Gove Peninsula in Northern Territory –
country of Yolngu People

Your homecoming in a flag-covered box
from Darwin, capital of a northern frontier
with its monuments marking the failure
of the Japanese to invade and
its heroic reconstruction after
cyclone Tracy. For the benefit of
the not-so-wealthy tourists, some galleries
sell indigenous art imitations.

Your cousin says you're too young to fly home
in a Cessna. Busloads of kids run wild,
twenty mothers wail in August dust. Sunlight
on bright fabric: reds and yellows. White ochre
on black skin. Clapsticks. Chanting. Another son
lost in a battle that won't go away.

Flight behaviour

1

Grey nomads and ecotourists escape
southern winters because they can. And
who hasn't thought, 'If only I could fly
away?' But why do animals migrate?
We see fantails; frail waifs on frail wings,
a thousand rufous avian splodges
fluttering across the benign sparkle
of Torres Strait. They're not called refugees,
they're not asylum seekers in frail boats.
So we shelve that sadness and muse on the
ideal of holidaying in Queensland.
An Outback Spirit bloke kneels to kiss this
extremity of the continent. More
of them will jet here from Cairns tomorrow.

2

How to know the crush or crash species? This
riddle encoded for fight or flight? And
who hasn't thought, 'If only I could fly
away?'
     In the local store, hoping for
one last flutter, a tropical display
of moths and butterflies pinned to corkboard.
Outside, people pinned down at New Mapoon;
pushed out of the old mission by bauxite.
Some try: the damned, the saved. It's in their genes.
Tibetans to Little Lhasa, Rohingyas
from Myanmar, IDPs* of Sudan,
Israelites out of Egypt, scraps queued for
maritime disasters, lines at borders…
Bombing has recommenced in Syria.

* IDPs are internally displaced persons.
In 1963, Tjungundji People were herded from the Presbyterian mission at Old Mapoon and forcibly moved to New Mapoon at the tip of Cape York by the Queensland Government to make way for expansion of the bauxite mine facility at Weipa. New Mapoon is the country of the Yadhaigana People; https://en.wikipedia.org/wiki/Mapoon,_Queensland

3

Across the sparkle of tropical sea,
so many tiny avian splodges.
Fantails like little butterfly scraps pinned
along migration maps. And who hasn't thought,
'If only I could fly away?' Benign waifs,
finding food and shelter. In recent years
met by Tjungundji stuck at New Mapoon;
driven by government from Old Mapoon.
And there's others, genetic coding shoves
them. Persecuted Iranians from
frail boats to be pinned down at Villawood.
Hindi pinned down by Hindi at their temple.
Tongan fruit pickers pinned down at Bowen.
Humanity, it's a flighty sort of word.

Villawood Immigration Detention Centre in Sydney is used to jail illegal immigrants; https://www.greenleft.org.au/content/visit-villawood-detention-centre-1

In 2001, the Sri Venkateswara Temple, Helensburgh, was found to have held stone masons from India as virtual prisoners for three years; http://www.cpa.org.au/z-archive/g2001/1036hind.html

Contract labour-hire companies entice Pacific Islanders and Malaysians with work visas, organise them to do fruit picking but then scam their wages; https://www.abc.net.au/news/rural/2017-11-01/exploitation-or-slavery-of-tongans-malaysians-in-horticulture/9102676

Slip slidin' away

Kutini-Payamu in Queensland – country of Kuuku Ya'u People
(including Kungkay and Kanthanampu Peoples).

Bird book says *raucous*; not so this morning.
Silence, the sound of palm cockatoos lofting,
their black wings beat us a sombre send-off.
Northern scrub-robins we leave you unseen;
book says *more information required*.
May your lowland rainforest keep you safe.
Our thanks to the red-cheeked parrot pair perched
on power lines and to the Lockhart River
mob for abiding our binoc-waving
intrusions.

        We brood and check lists. Was the
eclectus parrot everyone's favourite?
No! Green pythons don't count! Atlas page turned:
Wenlock, Portland Roads, Chilli Beach are gone.
The radio lifts our spirits. We feign
gladness until Simon and Garfunkel,
turned around and headed home again.

Dirty business

Lizard Island in Queensland – country of Mutumui and
Guugu-Yimidhirr Peoples

The footprints suggest the approach was more
inquisitive than voyeur and signal
a hasty retreat to where the person
averts his gaze toward the Coral Sea;
wondering perhaps about snorkels and
tropical explosions of colour. He
decides to wear spectacles when next
exploring the wild side of the island.

It's hot on the beach. The lovers collect
their sarongs and wander down for a swim.
They cover up to avoid sunburn and
the unsolicited nibblings of fish.
That bird is an oystercatcher, he tells
her. I'll give you oysters, she giggles.

Lord Howe Island

Red-tailed tropicbirds, mid-air on cliff edge
updrafts, land precisely at their nest ledge,
regurgitate fish for their downy young,
then back to hunting in a depleted ocean.

Shearwaters crash to ground at night, waddle
to nesting burrows. Angelic terns quarrel,
flashing white in mottled sunlight under pines.
Woodhens hover at the edge of existence.

We were four middle-aged youths on push bikes,
screaming down the hills; rushing off on hikes,
singing *climb every mountain*. And swimming,
tennis, fishing, reading, eating, drinking.
Good grief! How we resolved all the world's flaws
as our thirst developed for saving nature.

Winter surfer

Stanwell Park in New South Wales – country of Dharawal People

Stare out from safety beach. A magic spell
a blink. Your mind's adrift, you're there again
with yellow malibu. And Mary Jane
the drug of choice made every ocean swell
a perfect breast. Bikini dreams you know
are safe. Not so wild surfs with crushing waves.
You watch: young men are pumping hard. You gaze.
Their feats'd kill you if you tried, although

you won't. Your feet will paddle, hang about
with seaweed. An old salt; a retiring
beach-cast man with calcified thoughts. Alone,
the sandy swash covers your steps without
a trace. While fresh prints will appear in spring,
you're lost, and loneliness is all you own.

April 2121

Towradgi in New South Wales – country of Dharawal People

Just for the record, one hundred and one
years ago, we were not planning any
road trips. The car was good to go and so
were we, though the grandson had our camp light.
Could have been packed and gone in an hour. But
the June trip to Queensland was cancelled, they'd
even closed their borders! We pretended,
of course, and played our favourite CDs
and mused. At beer-o'clock, pandemics joined
the list of banned topics. The photo shows
us playing mah-jong at the camp table
in our front yard; tent cramped between bushes,
cast-iron pot simmering over a small fire.
Complacent smiles belie our anxiety.

White house

Kiama in New South Wales – country of Dharawal People

White roof of neatly folded iron
the pearly white walls and a sign
white message stick with dark intent
NO TRESPASSERS KEEP OUT you've said.
Ambiguous, your words in white.
Could they mean welcome in? Yeah right!
Our joke. You win. We'll not come near.
Your sign's intent is crystal clear.

White house of shame you oversee,
with all your white supremacy,
lands cleared of blacks and forest tall
yet crossed by convict-built stone walls.
Do you wonder what sign awaits
the likes of you at the Pearly Gates?

Tree change, sea change

February 2020, South Coast of New South Wales – country of Yuin People

Grass, so fresh you could eat it, marches past
twistings of corrugated roofing iron,
a concrete slab and debris heaps that were
stables. It skirts singular paddock trees
whose skeletal remains point skyward:
'Behold, there is the answer!'

Grass, so green you want to mow it, edges
a burnt-out ute. Washed ashore, parrots and
bloated forms of two singed ponies and a
charred milking cow awaiting discovery
by children.
              Beached charcoal borders the
littoral forest where epicormic shoots
mimic flames up blackened trunks and chartreuse
cycad fronds rise from ash:
                            'What decimation?'

Port Arthur

Port Arthur in Tasmania – country of Paredarerme People

verseless words blight us:
> modern-day massacre
> (Gordon River)
> (Thylacine)
> penal colony
> corporal punishment
> convicts
> sealers
> genocide
> British Empire
> Van Diemen's Land

some people:
> Martin Bryant – psychopath, mass murderer
> John Howard – gun law reformer
> Eric Reece – Tasmanian Premier
> George Robinson – preacher, Protector of Aborigines
> George Arthur – Lieutenant Governor
> Fanny Cochrane Smith – Palawa woman
> Truganini – Palawa woman
> James Cook – British explorer
> Abel Tasman – Dutch explorer

if our distress were to subside
we could visit you and then
the sonnet might make itself known

The twitchers' guide to Christmas Isle

Bring binocs, bonnets, bathers, books and blinkers (see below). Now, Due to Covid, visitors are not allowed. No entry into Christmas Island is permitted (miners are exempt) but what you see is upthrust scraps of concrete from some under-sea volcanoes. Excavating phosphate made big holes. The national park is sixty-four per cent of Christmas Island. Birding may be slow, so go down to the Cove. And while you're swimming, gazing skyward, golden bosunbirds will float above (with red-tailed tropicbirds). No staring; locals' privacy's important. Keep an eye out (of those blinkers) for the boobies (brown, red-footed, Abbott's); also dark-skin Tamil children with incarcerated families, they are shy. No, do not search for red crabs or use binocs within sight of the detention centre. Cryptic birds endemic to CI include a goshawk, pigeon, swiftlet, white-eye; hawk-owls are nocturnal and extremely cute but if you're into night life you're too late, the CI pipistrelle will flit no more (it is extinct) with thanks to introduced and feral species: Yellow crazy ants, black rats, the cats and common wolf snakes (chooks abound but thought not to eat micro-bats). Do not relax; be vigilant for vagrants. This may help us at the ABF, the ADF and AFP. Do not train binocs on suspicious life forms. LBJs could turn from Little Brown Jobs to your last Look Before Jail. Diversity of butterfly fish may be more enticing than the birds. Religion is diverse with Muslims, Buddhists, Christians, Taoist and Confucianists (here Hinduists are rare vagrants) all coexisting peacefully with emerald doves. These gentle folk are disinclined to keep caged birds. The kestrel, noddy, herons, sparrows, terns are mostly easier to see than detainees. It's Flying

Fish Cove for your frigatebirds (the Christmas, great and lesser) (flying fish are rarely spotted and the flittermouse is, as we said, extinct); ID entails detailed investigation. Passports must be carried at all times. Australian passengers are aliens and will be subject to a close investigation while the plane refuels at Learmonth Base, near Exmouth, Western Aus.

And birders without blinkers or heard uttering 'the *Tampa*' are indefinitely detained.

Here's to Petrarch: XXXX

And now it's come to this, kiss-kiss, kiss-kiss;
the sonnet-wielding poet bids adieu,
Professor Jack Oats-Bonza says hooroo,
your logophile departs this wordy bliss.

Two insatiable urges drove him here:
cacoethes scribendi (his need to write)
and second, the perpetual plight
of thwarting thirst. It's come to this, drink beer!

There's other loves he won't eschew: red wine,
singing, grandkids, coffee and the Good Fight;
there's Shakespearean sonnets, the Missus,
rhyming couplets and quoting the Yeats's line,
lovely's *but a brief dreamy kind delight.**
Perfection is beery cold wet kisses!

---

* From 'Never Give All the Heart', W.B. Yeats

Sunshine after days of rain

Sunshine after days of rain

houseboat-bound, their faces
that day-after-day-of-rain colour,
strung-out with the damp washing
left to their own devices, they slump and fiddle
tell limp anecdotes about school
without laughing
refuse to play board games
the radio issues flood warnings

the parents sing along
to another hippy-era song,
the kids grimace, tune out
bored, bored, bored
no recharge, very cranky

until sunlight jolts them onto the deck

Moorings

in Yeomans Bay all is perfect, perfectly still
and still the horizon saunters to and fro
among trees framed in our windows

until the pattern is broken by some rogue gust
mariners call them bullets but we trust
our mooring as we spin a full three-sixty

(after our little holiday, on the car radio
the Christchurch massacre is breaking news
our mood swings one-eighty to low low)

was the yeoman of our bay a shackled convict
or Kuringgai local, harvesting oysters
today the bay is ours

we read willingly and want to enjoy the author
but why does she knot raw metaphors
when we choose each word carefully

because once said, never lost
and one-down begins same as one-across
beware the anagram who sat / was hot / so what

it's just a crossword
we've heard
life is a puzzling foreplay

does it matter that the hue will
escape before it's caught
by the colouring pencil

ripples caress the hull (metaphor!)
and after, we jump overboard, cool
climb out, dry off

the wine is poured; we toast
our four hundred and forty-fourth full moon
in all this freedom we are moored

The Affair

have you finished *The Affair*
you ask me in a voice too loud
for the confines of the café
whereupon our table
one or two other friends
and acquaintances at other tables
as well as friends of friends
and complete strangers
see you nestle beside me
with a knowing grin because
it was you aroused my interest
and you've seen how it ends
but no one else in the café knows
you're talking TV
so all of them turn their heads
and their puppies
well behaved on their leashes
turn their heads
and all ears
listen up

Suburban birding

Brown goshawk
species #37 for my morning walk.
Alarm calls from other birds informs and stirs
me and *New Holland honeyeaters*.

Royal spoonbills
six slooshing with black-spoon mandibles
as they edge along Bellambi Lagoon.
And from the dense scrub on the dune
eastern whipbird
just one call heard.

Sooty oystercatchers
(wondering what the catch is?)
stalk those sessile crustaceans
with a whistle and a lot of patience.
Anyway I lied
there was none on the rock platform because of high tide.

The *English or common blackbird*
rhymes with turd.
Turdus melura in scientific jargon
blacklisted for its destruction in my vegie garden.

Yellow robins' piping song in our bushcare site,
yellow thornbills unusually quiet
moaning *yellow-tailed black-cockatoos*
spotted doves' annoying coos
little wattlebirds chase *house sparrows*
common starlings on wires in rows.

Masked lapwings will attack in spring; you'd call them *plovers*
galahs it's said are faithful lovers.
Superb fairywrens are known as flying gonads
to the ornithological grads.

Acridotheres tristis (the *mynah* birds) are much maligned
but they help clean up the park, so don't be unkind.
Call them common by name but desist
from calling them Indian if you're trying to be racist.

Rainbow lorikeets are colourful and
in black and white the *willy wagtail, pee wee, magpie, pelican*.

The *dollarbird* oddly quark-quark-quarks in rolling flight
but the best bird this morning was the rare *square-tailed kite*.

Seagulls gather

Shared lunchtime on the asphalt.
Maths, English and Science survivors
chew on canteen junk or white bread from home;
wrappings discarded, 'Snot mine, Miss,
I didn't 'ava pie today, honest, Miss.'
Crusts are discarded and Sir won't bother;
he's heard it all before,
'we're jest feedin' the starvin' birds, Sir.'
Sir prefers the perfumed ranks of the senior girls,
leaves Miss to supervise
the half-hearted handball until the bell,
the sweat-stench from synthetic uniforms,
the last reluctant boys grumbling into class
as they pause to watch the seagulls gather.

The last two lines given me by Ron Pretty from his memory of Keira High School and reimagined by me decades later.

Forest after fire

Endrick River and Quiltys Mountain, spring 2020
For Meggles and Nick, Olivia and Finn

decimated
is our word
for no green visible
no bird song
our bemused horror

recovery
is our hope
for a normal forest
including snakes
yes! we want snakes

we wince
at their collective agony
dare-not believe that a Creator
designed wombat burrows
as subsoil arks

black poles
stripe the skyline
others criss-cross the forest floor
in charcoal lines
holding treasures

regrowth
flame-tipped green shoots
from blackened trunks
blackened ground
blackened rocks

exfoliation
scars the sandstone plateau
but the ancients'
arrangement of stones
remains intact

black-footed
white cockatoos squawk at
last year's tenement
then waft on a breeze
like discarded title deeds

lyrebirds
till carpets of wattle seedlings
mauve orchids
ten centimetres above the ground
are the tallest flowers

an echidna!
the fire roars
we gape and gasp
it waddles downslope
the river! the river!

breathing holts, then
smoke illusions clear away
in the dusk
swimming freely
platypus

kangaroo prints
bless bare earth patches
resprouting grass is nibbled
multiple brands spruik
froggies-go-a-courting

Spotted a pardalote

Peter Potter, very keen bird spotter:
spotted doves, harriers and ducks, spotted
catbird, bowerbird and cryptic quail-thrush.
At an outback spot in the evening hush
doing a spot of wishing-on-a-star,
he wished instead for a spotted nightjar.
Peter Potter knew a spot from a dot;
thought the speckled warbler more spotted than not.

Peter Potter took his bird mania
and away he went to Tasmania;
for he knew Bruny Island to be best
to satisfy his desperate quest
for tiny forty-spotted pardalotes.
Then he'd have forty winks, go home and gloat.
From dawn to sunset his search was in vain.
Striated pardalotes drove him insane

with their *chipper chipper* call. Besotted
though he was with seeing forty spotted
pardalotes, at the Threatened Species Store
Peter Potter cried, 'There is nothing more
I want than a forty-spotter – please help!'
He found curios made from local kelp,
King Island cheese, pet thylacines and lots
of cuddly toys. Yes! Some had forty spots.

Buddha and the sherry drinkers

The Buddha happened upon
my mother and mother-in-law
having a contemplative sherry.

Good evening ladies,
tell me about Worry.

Gwen said, if you're not worried,
you don't know what's going on.

May said, you die if you worry,
you die if you don't,
so why worry?

Ah!
Just as I thought, said the Buddha,
The Middle Path.

Three glasses raised.
Bless you, ladies.
And cheers to you, Buddha.

Trekkers' horseman, Bhutan

thirty years young
tall, wiry, mute

two free hands
left foot angled twenty degrees inward
wearing light canvas shoes
bulky Western-style pants
several hand-me-down coats

gaining ground by mid-morning
gliding past
with a slight limp
slow nod, smile
tilt of chin
to indicate the way up the track

pointing and beaming at
sky crowded with blue
dotted with Himalayan griffon
edged by white peaks

going ahead with clop on rock
his eight-pony carrier team
their leader, the stoutest
with the best, red-tasselled headdress

The Fat Friar

The stop is outside the cleverly named fish and chip shop on the outskirts of the city. A zebra in a balloonish onesie and a tubby brown bear struggle onto my bus. Each has a two-year-old in a stroller. Mother zebra fiddles with a pink love-heart-covered smart phone, her tiny podgy hands almost dainty below the dozens of jingling bangles on her outsized wrists. A drab blonde ponytail swishes across a partially exposed tor of back and shoulders allowing a glimpse of tattoos; notably, a school of freshly coloured starfish are riding a wave of flesh from her left breast, around her chins and neck, finally disappearing under her hairline. My guess is, she once had a shaved head and an interest in marine biology. The sun, making its first appearance this week, beams brightly on zebra's face. It glints on nose rings, acne and facial hair. Deloris sleeps snug and silent in her stroller while her mother giggles with the bear across the aisle.

Michael is now out of his stroller and climbing on mother bear while he finishes his breakfast of two large lollypops, one per hand. Her sensibly short auburn hair, clear complexion and bottle-bottom spectacles are being smeared with honey-flavoured saliva. She laughs and licks her boy's sticky fingers. She is tightly covered by a woolly jumper and matching pull-up trousers. Bending at the waist while sitting is impossible due to her bulkiness. So, while maintaining her lively gossip with the zebra, she stands to lift Michael back into his stroller. She sits and stretches her legs across the aisle. Pooh Bear socks! Nice.

The bus jolts and Deloris wakes with a piercing squeal, which makes the zebra jump and giggle. Michael is yelling because he is sitting on his toy dog and has dropped his dummy on the floor. He blurts and sniffles then coughs a host of viruses for all to share. Bear replaces dummy in his mouth. The bus stops and they're right to go.

I thank the driver and alight with them. It's four stops early for me and his eyes are questioning but I don't care. I will walk briskly the long way to work and I will cancel my luncheon date. My New Year's resolutions are to remain childless, anorexic and miserably judgemental and also to take long walks in sunshine.

Zebra and bear have decided on cake and coffee at the Gloria Jean's next to the bus stop. After that, they'll check for special offers in the food hall then return on the bus because the kids really enjoy fish and chips for lunch.

Dawn chorus in the Cardiac Stepdown Unit

1 Repetitive calls

The slow
    dwonng
        dwonng
            dwonng
is the bedridden patients' alarm call.

The plastic do-dads in the overhead track
of the Haines Disposable Curtain slide
    swishy
        swish
            shhhh
like a twitcher sneaking up for a closer peek.

The skitty
    clickerty plickerty
        clickerty plickerty
            clickerty plickerty
of a lyrebird imitating the obs trolley.

From a far corridor, an unidentified
    bing bong
        bing bong
            bing bong

Bellbirds

    ping

                          ping

            ping

ping

                               ping

as the lifts deliver the morning shift.

2 Cacophonous outbursts

The morning shift!
Photocopies whir to life.
Outside, the continuous buzz of traffic. Infrequent *honks*.
Industrial-strength vacuum cleaner sucks and shrills.

3 Mixed flock chatter

'Blood sugar 5.2 that's good at 92.'
Loud hiccough from bed seven.
'Dialyse? What meds's he on?'
Mrs G in bed five breaks wind.
'Dress the groin? You'll be right, darlin.'
The drawn-out groan suggests otherwise!
'Not much of you. Bowels move this morning?'

4 Broken-hearted warbler

The cleaner busies
    a-zing
            a-zing
                    a-zing
chatters and fusses
    ah-pish
            ah-pish
                    ah-pish
She's youthful and kindly.
I'll woo her with my beautiful song
and steal away her heart!

Here for work

I could be a worker ant.
Every morning, my team cleans
the same nest entrance;
each day, the same.

Our kind team leader
has me work outside;
breathing fresh air.

Builder ants deep inside the nest
brave closeness and dark narrow passages;
they know how to make rooms
for the queen to lay her eggs.

Workers who bring out rocks
for us to clear away,
speak in awe of the queen
and her consorts.

Soldier ants are fearless;
they're keen to die in battle.
If they're injured they're not so scary
and we help them back to the nest.

Scouts return laden with food;
their adventure tales
leave me breathless.

I could be a worker ant.
        Thus in a Centrelink queue, mused I

Creation pondered at the clifftop

'Like ants, words thrown from a clifftop can fall or float.
If they echo, they're assonants.' – From the *Handbook of Etymology for Myrmecologists*

In the beginning there was the word, ant.
The first ant, Adamant,
was thrown out for his
stubbornness and other design faults.
What hope for his descendants?

The fickle ants
rhyme prayer with affair
and sycophants
sing psalms
while marching to their death
sentences in praise of cliffs
or ants or words.

Fire ants
conspire with asps (sibilants)
to burn the books of truth.

Biting ants,
the bigots, irritants, pedants,
frighten kinder words away.
With their underlining red legs
they drag gentler ants to the stake.
Their mandibles chomp wholesome paragraphs
to red mush.
They don't debate. They masticate and take
their lack of angel wings for granted.

Random ants
assemble; contestants
with faith in storytelling.
Some speak of a distant past.
Others saunter back to meet
those coming forward; ambulants.

Friendly ants,
nurturants, say it's OK
simply to be.

Nervous ants,
the shy novices, singletons and hesitants,
hope to be taken up by phrases
that scuttle to regroup
around the question:
What came first, the ant or the cliff?

The answer to these semantics
is a parachute check before jumping
and always to be a participant.

'Saint, is ant; ants vie to be natives;
pissants will always be contemptible along with blind faiths,
which can bid ants but will never make life complete.'
From the *Handbook of Myrmecology for Etymologists*

Emu's four-and-twenty lamentation

Blackbirds, you did not sing
in a pie to delight a king.

You came with the rabbits
and incarcerated white men.

Blackbird with white man;
a double negative.

A black and white picture can
engender hatred.

You overran a country. Imagine
your green dales overrun with Emus!

That Emu can't fly, is evident.
White man leader, you are not heaven sent

but you glance over your shoulder
expecting angel wings.

Have you ever seen an angel
any colour but white?

White man leader you inferred slavery
is not part of history.

History lesson: where genocide is only partial
slavery is the attendant evil.

Cooking lesson: Slaves desiring liberty
should beware gifts of pastry.

The humble pie is in need
of a new recipe.

Sergeant Small

I went broke in Shellharbour in 1981,
at the bowling club with Russell, playing the pokies, having fun.
Well I bludged another beer and saw his mateship wearing thin;
broke and cut and now I'm stuck with Hannah's hairy grin.

Desperation overcame me and I had to be alone,
I remembered me transportation, 'It's the Kingswood that you own.'
All over the road through Warilla, the coppers had a ball,
'A drunken defective Holden,' came the voice of Sergeant Small.

Oh I wish I was about twenty stone with a very nasty manner,
I'd go back to Shellharbour Bowling Club and beat up Russell Hannah.

The magistrate was kind to me, me licence took away.
He said, 'maybe this will help to cure your drunken driving ways.'
So if you're in Shellharbour, let me tell you it's no lie:
stay away from Hairy Hannah or you'll go for DUI.*

Oh I'm never gunna be twenty stone and I'll never have a nasty manner,
So next time I'm down Shellharbour way…
perhaps I could have a coffee
or a lemon squash with me old mate Russell Hannah.

* driving under the influence of alcohol

A parody on 'Sergeant Small,' which was written and recorded by Tex Morton in 1938 and subsequently banned. Incidently, it was Russell, not me, done for DUI!

For Paul on his sixtieth birthday

Don't be shocked to hear the gist of this tale,
the hex of the hexagenarian male
is not so much going steadily madder
but rather, the tightening of the bladder.

Now on alpine treks you must stay hydrated,
thus minus-ten-degree nights you'll be fated
to leave your warm tent. In the dark that's tricky
with bursting bladder and cold shrivelled dickie.

But here is salvation, a simple device
a marvellous asset; each night use it thrice.
The envy of trekkers from near and from far,
the humble, essential, amazing pee jar.

Butterflying

You give me butterflies	right inside my tummy
when you look at me	there's this feeling
my colours shine	I'm stripped and
your eyes glint	your power
over me	builds

until

my wings

whirl

earth

gives way

and

we soar together	my ambivalence
resolved	emerging
fearless	I'm afraid

My friend

For Nicole

My friend says her boy is amazing.

My friend says her boy is amazing
-ly messy sometimes
then her frustration shines
as she grinds with her teeth
and she purses her lips.

My friend says her boy laughs at jokes same as her;
and amazingly, messages her with a gag
when she's missing him most and she's
needing a lift.

My friend, with a glint in her eye,
says that loving her boy
is as easy as pie.
She is still quite amazed
that a bit of her life became him.
Over years she has cried every time he grew
up a bit more and he needed her less
but for handouts and hand-ups. And how can they
go their own way having undone the apron strings?

My friend shines amazing when
sometimes, she says
of her boy,
he's my friend.

Shepherd with ute

For Princess Jill of Illourie

The sheep are hundred-dollar notes blowing down the long paddock.* There's a tinge of green about this warm dawn.

Sheep are skittish. In this wind they're more skittish. Out of their bare paddock, they munch frantically at the low green pick among of browned-off clumps. They've stopped at the corner, twenty metres before the ute. They cannot be trusted.

The local train line opened in 1901 and in a vote of confidence, it stopped carting sheep the year we arrived. We're still here twenty-five years on. Pity the old siding is disused, the whole mob could be loaded up and sent off to Homebush. Pleasant little train ride through the Blue Mountains before they arrive at the abattoirs.

Crows angle and flap across the dusty air calling *carrr*. 'It's a ute, you murderous bastards,' I shout. They peck out the newborn lambs' eyes…black crows…stinging eyes…sleepless nights…eyes closed against the dust.

You catch forty winks when you can.

Our tree plantings have grown and there are many more small birds around the farm. Honeyeaters love the bottlebrushes and mistletoes. *Shit a brick*, one of many calls of the white-plumed honeyeater, is exactly what I think when my eyes snap open to see the sheep well down past the ute. They've caught me napping and tippy-toed by. I use my weary sheepdog limp to walk past them. They move to the grassy verges of the potholed narrow

---

* An authorised route for moving stock; a travelling stock route. This one also has an abandoned rail line through it.

tar strip that is our main road. The leaders reluctantly turn and chomp their way back toward the ute with me barking and clapping, mostly for my own benefit.

Gritty eyes wander to the horizon behind the house. Thankfully, our mountain, really only a big hill, was never cleared. The trees are splodges of green mottled with blue, grey and brown; you can feel the shade from a mile away. Our spring rises there but if it dries in this drought we'll be buying truck-loads of water again.

Time for the mob to go back to their paddock. The ute splutters and they look up. They know the routine and they're ready to head back for a drink and a bit of shade.

The sheep are fifty-dollar notes straggling through the long paddock like they've blown in from the insipid yellow-grey western horizon. The wind is all heat and dust.

(To bring a smile, add water, then swap the first and last paragraphs.)

Old currency

in those times
motorists on the dirt road
to the crossing
stopped
got out
swung open the wooden gates
checked for trains
drove across the lines
got out
closed gates
back in car
drove away

motorists might have passengers
sometimes the gates were too awkward
for women and children
(see Verse 1)

motorists might be lucky
if an enterprising youth
swung the gates
thus saving the motorists
the trouble of Verse 1

motorists cap-doffing or friendly-waving
had their number noted
and on their next crossing
the enterprising youth
could be seen
busy with his pushbike
(see Verse 1)

motorists of the very doffy-toffy type
might find a rerun of Verse 1
included a gate hinge jammed
and an enterprising youth
politely holding spanner and grease asking
'whatcha reckon it's worth
to fix it for ya?'

motorists might be spared Verse 1
for a copper or two
but the enterprising youth
considered this *infra dig*
he'd tell them
'a trey makes me day,
railway tracks rhymes with zacks
and lemonade's a bob a bottle'

Gardening list

ladybugs on our
cucumber vine, lazing skinks,
wrens perched on clothes line,
wondering the chance of rain;

chillies growing ready
for jam, jealous lorikeets
defending nectar
flowing from grevilleas;

like 'Scarborough Fair',
parsley, sage, rosemary, thyme,
fragrant lavender,
the tremble of rose petals;

perfume of fresh earth
ready for lettuce seedlings,
lawn tinged pink under
flowering callistemons;

shy white lilies edge
granite stepping stones, in shade
maidenhair-fern by
our joyous tubby Buddha;

arty clay toad stools
befriend gnomes in gay colours,
much else left to fate
while we contemplate our lot

Locally

1 Talking through the fence with my friend Hudson

His confidence
is grounded in a lifetime
of doing impossible yoga poses,
winning with a smile
(or strategically timed tear)
and his startling erudition.
All this at two years old.

2 People-watch along the cycleway

The toddler is smug in her pram,
fluffy puppies lead children,
someone else's grandparents sit at the playground,
strangers exchange a nod,
the busload of Samoans spills onto the beach,
a biker stops and sees surfies wipeout,
a young mum fusses at the bottom
of the slippery-dip, a young bloke eyes her tattoo,
all smile.

3 From the veranda

Crimson rosellas feed on purple fruit of dianella,
magpies warble over the drone of neighbourhood air-cons,
the real tomato taste of home-grown,
freshly brewed coffee,
beckoning chairs and goodness books,
Sculthorpe's solos for piano,
coronas and limes,
rhymes and later, merlot.

Omniserpent song

For Star and Izzi

Once upon all the times of everywhen,
you, the many Snake with hugging proclivities,
were led from paradise everywhere
into one language and said to be
Earth's everything:
the gentle little chiddles,
their mothers, all the mothers
and their babies growing to be
love makers, lore keepers, lusty
warmongers with trusty spears,
the sharpening grooves, sinuous valleys,
mountain spines; and
all the colours
from first beginnings; and
the gift of water

Rain brings green
and golden wattle
seen against indelible dye
of blood on bluest sky
brightened by your Rainbow,
so
all the spears can be rested
all the skins can be shed
all constricting turned to embracing

Written like this, have your many myths
lost their potency, their currency
gone for a song, maybe?
No!
Always you are
Everybody's Rainbow

Girter makes four prayers

After reading *Precipice* by Toby Ord (Hachette Books, 2020)

While girting in the salty air
I thought I'd try my hand at prayer
and so as not to be refused,
for twice the chance, both hands I used.

1

So please the gods, keep viral spread
and other nasty germs of dread
away from me and all my friends;
we promise we will make amends.

2

So please the gods to grow brown hairs
on snow leopards and polar bears
for camouflage in frostless clines
of zoos with elephants and lions.

3

So please the gods to disinvent
all fission, fusion, those intent
on blowing us to Kingdom Come
where angels be, their harps to strum.

4

So please you gods, the game down here
is out of hand. Send us some cheer
or miracle to make us dance.
Robotics may be our last chance!

Dear Weatherbeaten

Writers generally agree, '…weather can be quite unreasonable,' as you so aptly put it in your letter. My belief is, long ago, in a faraway land called Paradise, days were 70F; gentle afternoon zephyrs teased shiny chocolate skins until shower time, which was mid-afternoon. The grateful greenery soaked up the rain and the sun set in pink-warm dry air. Night skins gleamed in snuggly 60F moonlit climatological stasis. The Weather occurred at Elsewhere. One day, rainy showers came not to Paradise, which was a stochastic act of Who-knows; the glabrous ones complaining, 'What's happened to weather?' Unfortuitously for them, the Weather came to investigate, discovering that it was, and it was that: the centre of everything, provided it was variable and unpredictable and occasionally very nasty. Soon after the ascendency of the Weather, regressive variants evolved: (i) predictable, variable, occasionally very nasty – the Virus; (ii) predictable, static, occasional – the Politician.

If you require science regarding the vagaries of weather, do write to our meteorological columnist, Professor Bonza.

Sincerely and hooroofnow,
>the Poet
>XXXX

Laments due to:

Covid (2020)
The poet developed an ache
said, 'Lordy, my soul's yours to take.'
When next you share beers,
remember with tears
that nobody went to his wake.

Cancer (2021)
The poet, a rhythmic romancer,
was stricken with terminal cancer.
No time to rhyme lines
praising beers, spirits, wines;
a brief, living wake was his answer.

Chemo (2022)
The poet said, 'Here for the year,'
as his mates quaffed his wine, spirits, beer.
Give chemo its due,
all grog he eschewed
and the sober old sod is still here!

Acknowledgements

Madeleine Kelly is Senior Lecturer in Visual Arts at the University of Sydney and an internationally acclaimed painter. Her friendship is dear to me; her artwork for the cover of this book is a special gift.

Thanks to Star Woolley for assistance with the Indigenous language group names and place names associated with the sonnets. A few of the names were given me by local Indigenous people. Some names were gleaned from government literature and websites. All names were checked against the Australian Institute of Aboriginal and Torres Strait Islander Studies map at: https://aiatsis.gov.au/explore/map-indigenous-australia. This sometimes presented us with ambiguities that we resolved as best we could in a sincere attempt to acknowledge Indigenous nomenclature.

Thanks for all the encouragement and help from group meetings of South Coast Writers Centre poets, especially Kathleen Bleakley, Pat Farrar, Peter Frankis and Judi Morison; a poet needs like-minded mates and critical review! A poet also needs a patron to please, an ideal audience, a mentor, critical readers, copy editors and a Best Muse. Nicole Thomas, Amber Stewart, Ron Pretty, Pip Newall and Jean Clarke have excelled in their particular roles and often multitasked across roles. My collection of poems was much improved with their persistent support and I am privileged to have such brilliant and helpful mates.

A special thanks to the medical care workers who diagnosed and treated my cancer in 2021. In particular, rapid early diagnosis and referrals by my GP Steve Lyons, procedures by Robert Winn and rapid admission to a clinical trial at Wollongong

Hospital Cancer Care Clinic under the supervision of Daniel Brungs and care of (my new bestie) Chris Pobersnik, were key to extending my life. The clerical and nursing workers I have encountered have all been genuinely kind and truly professional. In particular, the nurses at the Cancer Care Clinic have taken the best care of me! What an amazing and privileged country we live in to have public facilities and workers delivering such a high standard of health care.

And finally, many thanks and much praise to Ginninderra Press for championing poetry in Australia. Ginninderra Press has strengthened my conviction and sense of worth as a poet.

'Grey honeyeater' was published in *Milestones*, Ginninderra Press (2021).
'Omniserpent song' was shortlisted for the South Coast Writers Centre 2021 Poetry Awards.
'Sonnet from the heart' was published in *I Protest! Poems of Dissent*, Ginninderra Press (2020).
'Joy', 'Locally', 'Flight behaviour', 'Sonnet from the heart', 'The Diamantina' and 'White house' were published in *Talking sheds and other corrugations*, BonzaBooks (2020).
'The Diamantina' was published in *Wild*, Ginninderra Press (2018).
'Resolve', 'Another dawn chorus', 'Requited love atop Lady Barrington', 'Silence' and 'Winter surfer' were published in *Soaring*, Ginninderra Press (2017).

A dedication

Jean Clarke has read and reread every written word I have drafted for publications; this book, my two previous books of poetry, my many published scientific articles. She has done so with a super-critical sense of correctness (factual, political, grammatical, style…). Before Jean, I could barely read, let alone write; she taught me and inspired me to write. Now we could argue for a week over the placement of a semi-colon! But we don't; I have them sorted! My passion for writing I owe to my Jeannie; I pay with gratitude and all my love.

www.ingramcontent.com/pod-product-compliance
Lightning Source LLC
Chambersburg PA
CBHW070924080526
44589CB00013B/1417